ESPECIALLY FOR DONNA

Bob Holloway

Paintings By Bob Holloway

Edited By John Holloway

All rights reserved. No part of this book may be reproduced without prior written permission of Bob Holloway, excepting brief quotes for purposes of a review

Copyright 2000
Printed in the United States

Published by Leathers Publishing

The Legend

The legend began with a fourth century archbishop of Myra, Turkey, who dedicated his life to good deeds and gift giving.

The Protestant Reformation tried to eliminate the veneration of saints, but the children held on to St. Nicholas and called him: Pere Noel in France — Father Christmas in England and Kris Kringle in Germany.

In America, the Dutch colonists simplified St. Nicholas to Sinter Klaus and then to Santa Claus.

The jolly old elf with a sleigh pulled by reindeer is an American invention and the legend goes on.

Let me show you Bob Holloway's Christmas Collection.

Hickery Dickery Dock.

The mouse ran up the Christmas clock.

To see if the star shining bright was signaling the birth of the true light.

To see if Old St. Nick's arms were going round to the hour when gifts and love abound!

THE BALLOON

AROUND THE WORLD IN 24 HOURS?

THE NUTCRACKER

Don't miss the angel!

THIS JOLLY OLD NUTCRACKER
HAS A SPECIAL NUT TO CRACK.
HE TELLS THE OLD, OLD STORY
TO KEEP US ALL ON TRACK.

THE COWBOY SANTA

Singing Santa

This jolly ole fellow knows all the right songs!

WHISPERS

WHISPER, WHISPER, GIVE ME
A CLUE,
WHAT DO YOU WISH FOR CHRISTMAS
WHAT SHALL I GIVE YOU?
SING ME A SONG
THE CAROL OF THE BELLS
DING DONG, DING DONG.
TO GIVE A GIFT AT CHRISTMAS
IS TO REMEMBER
THAT GREATEST GIFT OF ALL,
A TINY BABE SO TENDER.

A SIDEWALK SANTA

SANTA MOUSE

THE PARTRIDGE

THE EMPORIUM

"THE BOY PEEKING IN THAT WINDOW GREW UP TO BE THE EDITOR OF THIS BOOK."

"IN A VERY TALL TREE"

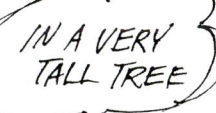

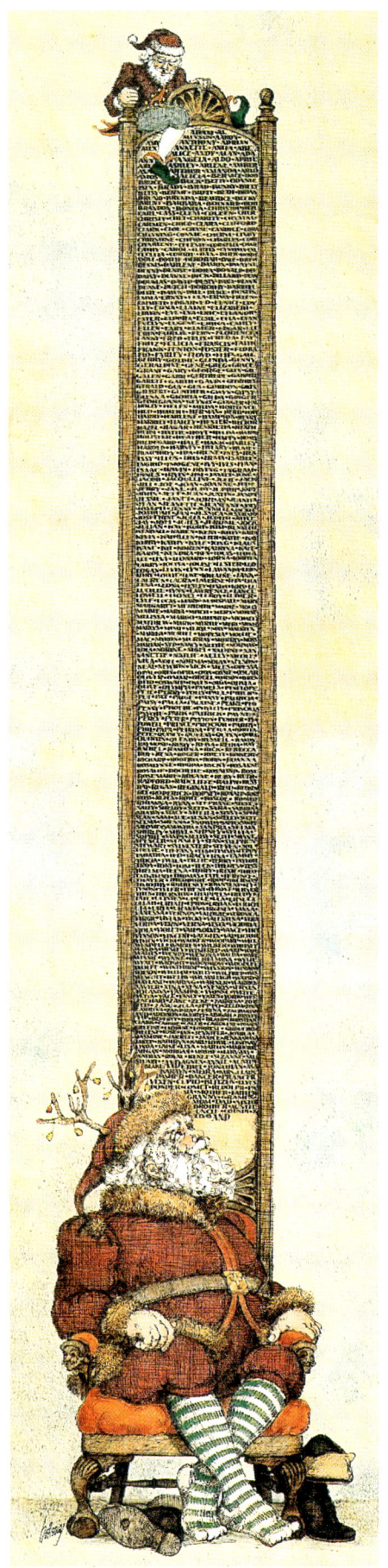

Santa's Christmas List

NOW, IF YOUR NAME ISN'T ON THE LIST, THERE'S ROOM AT THE BOTTOM UNDER "AND." BETTER ADD YOURS QUICK.

CHRISTMAS CHEST

THE WOODCARVER SANTA

Santa, Santa,
Carve away & make a
Nativity for display
With all the gifts
for fun and play
So we will remember
It's Jesus' day!

WOODCARVER III

*It's time to recall
that greatest gift
of all
So we dance with joy
with a gift for
each girl and boy*

"They obviously shop at different stores."

The Bag Lady Meets the Woodcarver Santa

CHRISTMAS TREE

IT WAS THE EVE OF
CHRISTMAS
AND THE HOUR WAS WEE
THAT I DREAMED OF A SANTA LAND
AND IT WAS A CHRISTMAS TREE.
IN A WINDOW I DID PEEK...
THE TREE I DID CLIMB TO SHOP,
BUT THE GREATEST GIFT
OF ALL
I FOUND IN THE TREETOP!

THE DOLLS

LUKE II

It's the Christmas story from the 2nd chapter of Luke on her sleeves and ending on the bottom of her skirt with the nativity pictured on her skirt.

NOEL

THE DOLL HAS THE CHRISTMAS CAROL "THE FIRST NOEL" MUSIC ON HER DRESS. YOU'LL ALSO FIND HER IN THE ARMOIRE WITH A NATIVITY AND SOME DICKENS CHARACTERS AND AN ANGEL, NOT TO MENTION A VERY SEXY LADY.

MORE DOLLS

THE DOLLS SHOWN ON THESE PAGES ARE FROM THE MARY HOLLOWAY DOLL COLLECTION. A DOLL MAKER CREATED THE SECOND GUY FROM THE LEFT AS THE HOLLOWAY SANTA.

HERALDS

THIS LITTLE ANGEL SINGS WITH THE HERALDS OF OLD OF THE WONDER OF WONDERS AS THE CENTURIES UNFOLD

THE STORYTELLER

THIS OLD GUY HAS A LOT OF GREAT TALES TO TELL INCLUDING DICKEN'S CHRISTMAS CAROL.

Another Great Storyteller

Starting at the top, it's London, the Christmas Carol and Great Expectations! Then, the Artful Dodger is picking Oliver's pocket and Oliver is picking Dickens' pocket. David Copperfield, The Old Curosity Shop and The Tale of Two Cities at the bottom.

THE CHRISTMAS BUG

Been there, done that.

SANTA'S MAILBOX

I'D CALL THAT EXPRESS MAIL FOR SURE!

THE ANGELS

ANGEL I (BELOW)
LEADS THE SHEPHERDS TO BETHLEHEM

ANGEL II (LEFT)
LEADS THE WISE MEN TO BETHLEHEM

ANGEL III (NEXT PAGE)
THE DESTINATION

THE NATIVITY ANGEL

THE BUTTERFLY ANGEL

Ever been kissed by a butterfly?

NOEL ANGEL

HEELS AND HOSE? SHE MUST BE THE PERFORMANCE ANGEL.

THE GUARDIAN ANGEL
WITH THE CHILDREN OF THE WORLD

PLAZA LIGHTS

THE COUNTRY CLUB PLAZA
KANSAS CITY, MISSOURI

THIS CHRISTMAS LIGHTING-EXTRAVAGANZA HAS A 70-YEAR HISTORY. THE MOORISH ARCHITECTURE LENDS SO MUCH TO THIS LIGHTING SPECTACULAR FROM THANKSGIVING EVE INTO THE NEW YEAR.

BETHLEHEM HOTEL

THE ELF BAND

> WONDERING WHAT THAT MUSICAL INSTRUMENT THE SECOND ONE FROM THE RIGHT IS? IT'S A GUT BUCKET FROM THE OZARKS.

For Information on Future Publications: Bob Holloway's Bible Stories Collection and Bob Holloway's Patriotic Collection visit:

www.bobholloway.com

email: bob@bobholloway.com

Bob Holloway's Christmas Collection

Bob Holloway Studio & Gallery
12223 Avila Drive
KCMO 64145
816-942-2336

Published by Leathers Publishing
4500 College Blvd.
Leawood, KS 66211
888-888-7696

Bob Price Holloway

Bob Price Holloway was born in Centralia, Missouri in 1928 and was raised in nearby Columbia. In 1942, partially as a result of World War II, the family moved to Kansas City. Here, he attended Westport High School and his interest in art blossomed under the tutelage of teacher Shelton Wilhite.

While still attending high school, Holloway received on-the-job training in the commercial art department at Western Auto Supply, Co., then headquartered in Kansas City. In 1954, he moved on to become an advertising agency art director. In this capacity he received many Art Director's Club awards for both print and television advertising throughout his career. He also served as president of the Kansas City Art Director's Club. In total, Holloway spent 40 years as an art director and illustrator, eventually forming his own agency, and later Bob Holloway Studio and Gallery.

It was in 1952 that he participated in his first art fair. Since that time, the awards he has won for painting and drawing are too numerous to count. For 26 years he exhibited at the Country Club Plaza Art Fair, then moved on in 1979 to become co-founder of Art Westport as an opportunity for local artists who had been juried out of the other event. Ultimately in 1988 he retired from advertising to exhibit his work at shows across the country.

By the turn of the century he was exhibiting in some 40 shows each year, from Minnesota to Texas and from Arizona to Massachusetts. Through this participation he has seen his work purchased and displayed in such diverse places as Argentina, Australia, Canada, England, France, Greece, Italy, Luxembourg, Switzerland and countless others.

Holloway lives in Kansas City with his wife Mary. They have two daughters and one son.